RUSSELL GRADERS

PHOTO ARCHIVE

RUSSELL GRADERS
PHOTO ARCHIVE

Photographs from the
Higgins Collection of the
Shields Library, University of California, Davis

Edited with introduction by
P. A. Letourneau

Iconografix
Photo Archive Series

Iconografix
P.O. Box 18433
Minneapolis, Minnesota 55418 USA

Library of Congress Card Number 93-80438
ISBN 1-882256-11-5

93 94 95 96 97 98 99 5 4 3 2 1

Cover and book design by Lou Gordon, Osceola, Wisconsin
Digital imaging by Pixelperfect, Madison, Wisconsin

Printed in the United States of America

PREFACE

The histories of machines and mechanical gadgets are contained in the books, journals, correspondence and personal papers stored in libraries and archives throughout the world. Written in tens of languages, covering thousands of subjects, the stories are recorded in millions of words.

Words are powerful. Yet, the impact of a single image, a photograph or an illustration, often relates more than dozens of pages of text. Fortunately, many of the libraries and archives that house the words also preserve the images.

In the Photo Archive Series, Iconografix reproduces photographs and illustrations selected from public and private collections. The images are chosen to tell a story...to capture the character of their subject. Reproduced as found, they are accompanied by the captions made available by the archive.

The Iconografix Photo Archive Series is dedicated to young and old alike, the enthusiast, the collector and anyone who, like us, is fascinated by "things" mechanical.

ACKNOWLEDGMENTS

The photographs and illustrations appearing in this book were selected from the Higgins Collection of the Shields Library, Special Collections, University of California, Davis. We thank John Skarstad, Curator Special Collections, and his staff for their cooperation. Supplemental photographs (pages 45, 70, 71, 97-99) and reference materials regarding the history of the Russell Grader Manufacturing Company were provided by the Caterpillar Inc. Corporate Archives.

Russell Motor Highway Patrol No. 1, the industry's first motorized grader.

INTRODUCTION

In the first decades of the twentieth century, the demand for new and improved roadways grew in America as the number of cars and trucks increased. In 1921, the Federal Highway Act authorized more than $1 billion in federal funds for road projects. The development of the 2-lane interstate system followed and, with it, the market for road construction machinery boomed.

Russell Grader Manufacturing Company was one of the first American manufacturers to specialize in road grading equipment. Beginning in 1903 with horse-drawn machines, the company later developed equipment especially for use with tractors. In 1920, the introduction of the first motor grader firmly established Russell as the industry leader.

Russell Grader Company was founded in Stephen, Minnesota by Richard Russell and C.K. Stockland. Russell and Stockland developed a horse-drawn elevating grader with a gas engine-driven conveyor, the first such machine on the market. The prototype was built in the shop at Stockland's implement dealership, and early production was jobbed-out to the com-pany that supplied the conveyor. In 1906, as a way to lower the grader's cost, it was decided to bring manufacturing in-house. Additional investors were found and a factory was built in Minneapolis.

In the early years, Russell continuously struggled with problems related to the gasoline engines used on their machines. Initially, the conveyor was fitted with a 7 horsepower, single-cylinder Lansing engine. It proved unreliable and lacked sufficient power. It was soon replaced by a 10 horsepower, single-cylinder Valentine engine. It too proved inadequate. Consequently, the company chose to build larger engines of its own: a 2-cylinder, 14 horsepower unit, fitted to machines sold for township use; a 3-cylinder, 21 horsepower unit, fitted to machines sold for heavier road construction. While the larger engines proved more satisfactory, the improved grader's higher cost forced Russell to abandon the gas engine-driven conveyor and revert to a gear-driven system.

Russell survived these early problems only because the company had expanded its line to include low blade graders, drag scrapers, wheel scrapers, and plows. In 1908, a small 2-horse maintenance grader was the first new product added to the line. This was followed by the introduction of the first Simplex Road Machine, an 8-horse grader with 7-foot 3-inch blade. In 1908, Russell introduced the Traction Special, a grader especially designed for use with tractors. The Standard, Mogul, Special, and Reliance graders, larger machines built for use with increasingly more powerful tractors, soon followed.

In 1920, Russell introduced the Motor Hi-Way Patrol No. 1, the first self-propelled grader. It incorporated an Allis-Chalmers 2-wheeled tractor with a grader unit behind. Because of patent problems, Allis-Chalmers withdrew the tractor from the market and, in 1923, production of the Russell machine was suspended.

The concept of the motor grader had proved popular, and Russell soon developed new models. In 1925, the company introduced the Motor Patrol No. 2, powered by a Fordson tractor. Unlike the earlier machine, Russell placed the grader unit in front of the tractor. Because Fordson showed little interest in working with Russell, the Motor Patrol No. 2 was dropped in 1927. The Motor Patrol No. 3, based on McCormick-Deering's Model 10-20, was introduced in late 1925 and remained in production until 1929. In late 1926, Russell introduced the Motor Patrol No. 4, a motor grader unit fitted to the Caterpillar Two-Ton tractor. Five machines were sold in 1926 and, in 1927, 265 machines were sold. The Motor Patrol No. 5, introduced in 1927, incorporated the Cletrac K-20 tractor. The Motor Patrol No. 6, based on the Caterpillar Twenty, was the last motor grader in this early series.

In addition to graders, scrapers, and plows, Russell built wagons, drag lines, gravel crushers, screens, bins, and conveyors. The company also built the industry's first fully portable gravel screening and crushing unit, the No. 10 plant.

The popularity of the Russell Motor Patrol No. 4 did not go unnoticed by Caterpillar Tractor Company. In August 1928, Caterpillar successfully negotiated the purchase of Russell. Following the acquisition, Caterpillar sold the gravel equipment, drag line, and scraper lines to different companies. The Motor Patrol models that incorporated competitive tractor units were dropped, while the new Motor Patrol Models No. 10, No. 15, and No. 20, incorporating the Caterpillar Models Ten, Fifteen, and Twenty respectively, soon bore the Caterpillar name.

While the Russell name became a part of history, the innovative work done by the company was not lost. As early as 1927, Russell engineers had begun experimental work that directly influenced the design of the 1931 Auto Patrol motor grader, one of Caterpillar's most revolutionary and successful machines.

Russell Graders Photo Archive features photographs and illustrations of a variety of Russell machinery built or develop-ed prior to Caterpillar's acquisition of the company. For reference, we include specifications for a number of machines and a comprehensive list of grader serial numbers.

Russell Grader Manufacturing Company Minneapolis Headquarters. 1917.

A row of Russell graders in front of the factory. April 1926.

Russell plant employees pose in front of shops. June 1927.

The sales department clerical workers. May 1927.

Russell machine shop. March 1926.

Parts storage area. May 1927.

A carload of Russell Junior Graders in the shipping and receiving area. May 1927.

BLADE GRADERS,
ELEVATING GRADERS, AND PLANERS

RUSSELL JUNIOR GRADER

6 or 7-foot Blade.   For 4 Horses and 2 Men   May also be furnished with 8, 10 or 12-Foot Maintenance Blade

Weight 1550 Pounds

Best Results in Road Maintenance may be obtained by using the Russell Junior with 2 men and 4 horses or a small tractor. Two men (one driving, the other operating the grader) can do better work than one man doing both operating and driving. It may cost a little more than using a one-man grader but many experienced road builders contend that it pays in producing better and more uniform work. For light road building, digging ditches, crowning up old grades, cleaning out ditches, etc., the Junior will give excellent results. **An Engine Steering Pole is furnished** at a small additional expense. Gas tractors of 8 to 10 horse-power are best adapted in size for use with the Junior.

Specifications

Weight — 1550-lbs.

Blade — 4 sizes made of Special Carbon Steel.
        6-ft. long, 14-1/4-in. wide, 1/4-in. thick.
        7-ft. long, 14-1/4-in. wide, 1/4-in. thick.
        8-ft. long, 14-1/4-in. wide, 1/4-in. thick.
        10-ft. long, 15-1/4-in. wide, 5/16-in. thick.

Cutting Edge — Made of Special Carbon Steel.

Blade Beams — 3/4x3-in. flat.

Blade Braces — 1-in. round.

Blade Pitch Adjustment — 4 positions.

Blade Side Shift — 16-in.

Blade Lift Above Ground — 12-in.

Circle — 36-in. diameter, 3x3x3/8-in. "T" Steel.

Draw-bars — 3-1/2x2-1/2x3/8-in. angles. Draft spring in draw-bar.

Kingbolt — 1-1/8-in. round.

Method of Blade Lift — Worm Gear.

Lifting Links — 1-in., Special Carbon Steel. Adjustable.

Lifting Arms — 1-1/4-in., Special Carbon Steel.

Hand Wheels — 22-1/2-in. diameter. 1-in. rims.

Frame — 5-in. x 9lb. Channel. Supported by stiff braces.

Axles — Made of Special Carbon Steel.
        Front, 1-5/8-in. round. Rear, 1-5/8-in. square.
        Rear axle may be shifted to either side or adjusted pivotally.

Wheels — Flat or Flanged with Removable Boxes.
        Front, 26-in. diameter, 3-in. Tires, 8-1/2-in. bearings.
        Rear, 32-in. diameter, 3-in. Tires, 8-1/2-in. bearings.

Pole — Either Oak Horse Pole or Engine Steering Pole furnished.

Tread — Front, 37-in. Rear, 68-in.

Wheel Base — 100-in.

Scarifier Attachment — Weight, 125-lbs., Length, 53-in.
        Ten Teeth, 1-1/8-in. round, 13-in. long, spaced 5-1/2-in. apart.

The Russell Junior Grader, commonly sold as a two man, four horse grader, was introduced in 1912.

Junior Grader with 6-foot blade demonstrating road maintenance work. 1917.

Two teams of horses pulling Junior Graders. 1917.

A one man Junior Grader pulled by a team of water buffalo.

Fordson tractor pulling a Junior Grader.

Emerson-Brantingham Big Four "30" pulling a Russell Traction Special.

Emerson-Brantingham Big Four "30" and Russell grader building a sloping grade for a rural road project.

Emerson-Brantingham Big Four "30" trenching with a Russell Traction Special.

Hart-Parr "Old Reliable" pulling a Traction Special.

Avery 40-80 pulling a Traction Special Grader. Minneapolis. Circa 1918.

RUSSELL HI - WAY PATROL NO. 2

6, 7, 8 or 10-foot Blade. One Man - Two Horse Grader

Weight 1350 Pounds

This was the first Patrol Grader on the Market. While other patrol graders are now offered, and patterned after this model, we can say, positively, that the Russell Hi-Way Patrol is in a class by itself. Like the Larger Grader it has lifting arms with two bearings giving steady action. It has snug fitting joints throughout entire lifting mechanism, take-up bearings in worms (eliminating end play), lifting links that may be lengthened or shortened, shock spring in draw-bar, pole spring, long wheel base, large wheels, removable boxes and a comfortable seat with flexible spring. **The Smooth Cutting Action** with practically no vibration is due to the rigid construction of the Hi-Way Patrol. In working on gravel roads an ordinary patrol grader will not stand up. **An Engine Steering Pole,** similar to the one used on the Junior Graders, is furnished for those using a small tractor. The Hi-Way Patrol No. 2 and the Fordson tractor make a good unit. One man can easily control tractor and operate grader. **A Scarifier Attachment** that fits in front of blade may be furnished for light scarifying work.

Specifications

Weight — 1350-lbs.

Blade — 4 sizes made of Special Carbon Steel.
       6-ft. long, 14-1/4-in. wide, 1/4-in. thick.
       7-ft. long, 14-1/4-in. wide, 1/4-in. thick.
       8-ft. long, 14-1/4-in. wide, 1/4-in. thick.
       10-ft. long, 15-1/4-in. wide, 5/16-in. thick.

Cutting Edge — Made of Special Carbon Steel, 5/16-in. thick.

Blade Beams — 3/4x2-1/2-in Flat Bars.

Blade Braces — 1-in. round.

Blade Pitch Adjustment — 4 positions.

Blade Side Shift — 14-in.

Blade Lift Above Ground — 11-in.

Circle — 36-in. diameter, 3x3x3/8-in. "T" Steel.

Draw-bars — 3-in. x 2-in. x 5/16-in. angles.

Kingbolt — 1-1/4-in. round.

Method of Blade Lift — Worm Gear.

Lifting Links — 1-in., round. Special Carbon Steel.

Lifting Arms — 1-1/4-in. round.

Hand Wheels — 20-in. diameter. 1-1/4-in. rims.

Frame — 3-1/2-in. x 2-1/2-in. x 5/16-in. angle.

Axles — Made of Special Carbon Steel.
       Front, 1-3/8-in. round, 4-ft. 7-in. long.
       Rear, 1-5/8-in. round, 6-ft. 6-in. long.

Bearings — Front, 1-3/8-in. x 6-in. Rear, 1-11/16-in. x 8-1/2-in.

Wheels — With Removable Boxes, "screwed on" Hub Cap.
       Front, 24-in. diameter, 1/2-in. x 3-in. Tires.
       Rear, 32-in. diameter, 1/2-in. x 3-in. Tires.

Tread — Front, 46-1/2-in. Rear, 66-in.

Wheel Base — 100-in.

Scarifier Attachment — Weight, 125-lbs., Length, 53-in.
       Ten Teeth, 1-1/8-in. round, 13-in. long, spaced 5-1/2-in. apart.

RUSSELL HI-WAY PATROL NO. 3

6-Foot, 8-Foot or 10-Foot Blade. For 2 or 3 Horses - One or Two Men
Weight 1600 Pounds

A Better Built Patrol Grader. Heavy enough to do light ditch work and light enough to do maintenance or patrol work. The machine cannot be equalled by any other machine of its same size for smooth cutting due to the strong construction and snug fitting joints. **The Worm and Gear** are machined and have a take-up for wear in both gear and worm. Removable brass bushings are used in lifting arm bracket. The lifting links are of the ball and socket type. An adjustment is provided to eliminate all play in circle. All joints are surprisingly snug--no jumping or chattering over rough roads. **The Long Wheel Base**, large wheels with removable boxes and large bearings, shock spring in draw bar, pole spring, large platform and comfortable seat are some of the features found in the HI-Way Patrol No. 3. **Scarifier Attachment** that fits directly in front of blade may be furnished. The blade can be used independently of the scarifier. The scarifier being hinged can be lifted out of the way.

Specifications

Required H. P. — 2 and 3 Horses.
Weight — 1600-lbs.
Blade — Made of Special Carbon Steel. May be equipped with either
        10-Foot blade, 15-1/4-in. wide, 5/16-in. thick.
        8-Foot blade, 14-1/4-in. wide, 1/4-in. thick.
        6-Foot blade, 14-1/4-in. wide, 1/4-in. thick.
Blade Beams — 3/4-inch x 3-inches. Special Carbon Steel.
Lateral Adjustment of Blade — 10-inches.
Pitch Adjustment of Blade-4 positions.
Blade Lift Above Ground — 12-inches.
Circle — 3x3-1/2x3/8-inches. "T" Steel.
Circle Diameter — 36-inches.
Blade Braces — 1-inch round.
Cutting Edges — 5/16-inches thick.
Draw Bars — 3-1/2x2-1/2x3/8-inches angle.
Kingbolt — 1-1/4-inches round. Special Carbon Steel
Lifting Links — 1-inch round.
Lifting Arms — 1-5/16-inches round.

Method of Lifting Blade — Worm Gear, Cut Teeth.
Hand Wheels — 22-inch diameter — 1-1/4-in. Rims.
Frame — 4x3x3/8-inches angle.
Frame Above Ground — 41-inches.
Front Axle Size — 1-5/8-inches round
Rear Axle Size — 1-5/8-inches square.
Length of Front Axle — 4-feet, 10-inches.
Length of Rear Axle — 6-feet, 10-1/2-inches.
Lateral Shift of Rear Axle — 20-inches.
Pivotal Shift of Rear Axle — 15 degrees.
Diameter of Wheels — Front, 26-inches. Rear, 32-inches.
Tires — 3-inches x 1/2-inch.
Length of Bearing — 8-1/2-inches.
Tread — Front, 46-inches. Rear, 70-1/2-inches.
Wheel Base — 118-inches
Length Overall — 144-inches.
Scarifier Attachment — Weight, 125-lbs., Length, 53-in.
        Ten Teeth, 1-1/8-in. round, 13-in. long, spaced 5-1/2-in. apart.

The Hi-Way Patrol No. 2, a one man, two horse machine, was also suited for use with small tractors.

Rail car loaded with frames for the Highway Patrol No. 2. Built from 1923 to 1929, it was one of Russell's best selling machines.

RUSSELL STANDARD No. 1 GRADER

"A Light Standard" Weight 2300 Pounds

6-1/2, 7 or 8-Foot Blade with or without Scarifier. 4 to 6 Horses - 8 to 12 H. P. Tractor

(Formerly called Russell Badger Grader)

A Light Standard suitable for moderate grading or reshaping of old roads. The Standard No. 1 is a general all around grader as it may be used with animal power or a tractor. When a tractor is used for power an engine steering pole is recommended. Scarifier Combination Machine. It may be equipped with a scarifier ahead of the blade and both worked in combination or independently of each other. It will do a variety of work, light grading and maintenance work. It's an ideal machine for cities, villages and townships. Back Sloper Attachment is highly recommended. It will build a flat bottom ditch. Attached in a few minutes.

Specifications
Weight — 2300-lbs.
Weight with Scarifier Attachment — 2800-lbs.
Blade — 4 sizes, made of Special Carbon Steel.
        6-1/2-ft. long, 15-in. wide, 5/16-in. thick.
        7-ft. long, 15-in. wide, 5/16-in. thick.
        8-ft. long, 15-in. wide, 5/16-in. thick.
        10-ft. long, 15-in. wide, 3/8-in. thick.
        12-ft. long, 15-in. wide, 3/8-in. thick.
Cutting Edges — Special Carbon Steel.
        8-ft. and 10-ft. blades reinforced on back with angle.
Blade Beams — 7/8x3-in. flat bars.
Blade Braces — 1-1/8-in. round.
Blade Pitch Adjustment — 4 positions.
Blade Side Shift — 17-in.
Blade Lift Above Ground — 10-1/2-in.
Circle — 42-1/2-in. diameter, 3-1/2x3-1/2x1/2-in. "T" Steel.
Draw-bars — 4x3x3/8-in. angle.
Kingbolt — 1-1/4-in. round. Special Carbon Steel.
Method of Blade Lift — Worm Gear.

Lifting Links — 1-1/4-in. round, Special Carbon Steel.
Lifting Arms — 1-1/2-in. round.
Hand Wheels — 30-in. diameter. 1-5/16-in. rims.
Frame — 5-in. x 9lb. Channel.
Axles — Made of Special Carbon Steel.
        Front, 1-3/4-in. round. Rear, 1-3/4-in. square.
Wheels — Front, 28-in. diameter, Flat or Flanged, 1/2x4-in. Tires.
        Rear — 36-in. diameter, Flat or Flanged, 1/2x4-in. Tires.
Bearings — 1-13/16x10-in.
Tread — Front, 40-in. Rear, 69-in. Wheel Base, 129-in.
Scarifier Attachment
Weight of Block — 150-lbs. Steel Casting. Length of Block, 40-in.
Number of Teeth — 7.
Size of Teeth — 2-1/2x3/4-in. Flat, 21-in. long.
Spacing Between Teeth — 6-in.
Method of Lifting — Worm Gear.
Back Sloper
Blade for Cutting Ditch Bottom — 16-inches long.
Wing — 42-inches long. Weight — 225 pounds.

RUSSELL STANDARD No. 3 GRADER

"A Big Standard" Weight 3800 Pounds

8-Foot Blade. With or without Scarifier. For 8 Horses or 20 H. P. Tractor.
May be also furnished with a 10 - Foot or 12 - Foot Maintenance Blade.

A Heavy "Standard" built for heavy or moderate grading using a medium sized tractor or animal power. The Draft is Light--no heavier to pull than lighter machines with the same length blade. This is an ideal machine for city work as it may be used for scarifying hard macadam roads as well as grading and maintenance work. A combination Machine--The scarifier attachment fits in front of blade--all adjustments are made from the rear platform. Scarifier and blade may be operated together or independently of each other. Back Sloper Attachment--will build a flat bottom ditch. The Standard No. 3 was designed for a back sloper. Attached in a few minutes.

Specifications

Weight with Horse Hitch — 3500 pounds.
Weight with Engine Hitch — 3800 pounds
Weight with Scarifier Attachment — 4500 pounds.
Blade — 8-feet long, 17-1/2-in. wide, 1/2-in. thick.
      10-feet long, 17-1/2-in. wide, 1/2-in. thick.
      12-feet long, 17-1/2-in. wide, 1/2-in. thick.
Blade Extension — 2 or 3-foot furnished when so ordered.
Cutting Edge — Special Carbon Steel.
Blade Beams — 3-1/2-in. x 1-1/4-in.
Blade Braces — 1-3/8-in. round.
Blade Pitch Adjustment — 4 positions.
Blade Side Shift — 24-in.
Blade Shift Above Ground — 13-in.
Circle — 52-in. diameter, 4x4x1/2-in. "T" Steel.
Draw-Bars — 5x3x3/8-in. angle.
Kingbolt — 2-in. round.
Method of Blade Lift — Worm Gear.
Lifting Links — 1-3/8-in. round. Adjustable to suit work.
Lifting Arms — 1-3/4-in. round.
Hand Wheels — 30-in. diameter — 1-5/16-in. rims.
Frame — 6-in., 10-1/2-lbs. channel.

Axles — Front, 2-in. round, 10-in. x 2-in. bearing.
      Rear — 2-1/4-in. square, 10-in. x 2-in. bearing.
Wheels — Flat or flanged tires. 5-in. x 1/2-in. tire.
      Front, 30-in. diameter. Rear — 40-in. diameter.
      Removable boxes — Screw hub caps.
Tread — Front, 48-inches. Rear, 80-inches.
Wheel Base — 153-inches.
Scarifier Attachment
Weight of Block — 270 pounds (steel casting).
Length of Block — 44-inches.
Number of Teeth — 6.
Size of Teeth — 3-in. x 1-in., 21-in. long. (Special Carbon Steel).
Spacing of Teeth — 8-1/2-inches apart.
Lift Gear — Steel casting.
Lifting Links — 1-5/8-inches.
Draw-Bar — 4-in. x 1-1/8-inches.
Scarifier Clearance — 10-inches.
Back Sloper Attachment
Blade for Cutting Ditch Bottom — 21-inches.
Wing — 46-inches.
Weight — 450 pounds.

Russell Standard No. 1 Grader, originally designated the Badger, and a McCormick-Deering Model 10-20. March 1927.

The steering pole and control cables on a Standard Grader No. 1 and McCormick-Deering 10-20.

A horse-drawn Russell Standard with scarifier. Built from 1912 to 1925, it preceded the Standard No. 3.

RUSSELL SUPER - SPECIAL GRADER

8, 9 or 10 - Foot Blade. With or without Scarifier.
May also be Furnished with 12 - Foot Maintenance Blade.
For 18 to 20 Horse - Power Tractor or Animal Power

A Grader and Scarifier in One Unit. The scarifier and blade may be operated together or independently of each other. This combination machine is built like the Super-Mogul Scarifier-Grader except lighter in weight and smaller in capacity. Ideal Grader for both heavy grading and maintenance work where tractor is used for power. In other words the Super-Special is a general purpose grader. May also be used with Animal Power. The light draft makes it possible to use animal power when desired. Back Sloper--That will build a flat bottom ditch furnished when so ordered.

Specifications

Weight — With 8-ft. Blade and Engine Pole, 5,400 pounds.
With 8-ft. Blade and Horse Pole, 5100 pounds.
With Scarifier Attachment, 6,400 pounds.

Blade — Made of Special Carbon Steel. May be equipped with either
8-foot blade, 1/2-in. thick, 19-1/2 in wide.
9-foot blade, 9/16-in. thick, 20-1/2-in. wide.
10-foot blade, 9/16-in. thick, 20-1/2-in. wide.

Blade Extension — 2 or 3-foot furnished when so ordered.
Cutting Edge — Made of Special Steel.
Blade Beams — 3-1/2-in. x 1-1/2-in. Special Carbon Steel.
Blade Braces — 1-5/8-in. round.
Blade Pitch Adjustment — Four positions.
Blade Side Shift — 26-inches.
Blade Lift Above Ground — 15-inches.
Circle — Steel casting, 46-in. diameter.
Draw-Bars — 4-in. x 1-1/8-in. Special Carbon Steel.

Lifting Links — 1-1/2-in. round, Special Carbon Steel.
Lifting Arm — 2-inches. round, Special Carbon Steel.
Kingbolt — 2-in. round, Special Carbon Steel.
Frame — 7-in., 12-1/4-lb. channel, reinforced.
Axles — Front, 2-1/4-in. round, Special Carbon Steel.
Rear, Built-up Section with 2-1/2-in. spindle.
Bearings — 2-1/4-in. x 11-in.
Wheels — Front, 32-in. diameter, 6-in. x 1/2-in. tires.
Rear, 40-in. diameter, 6-in. x 1/2-in. tires.
Detachable Flanges.
Method of Lifting Blade — Worm Gear.

Hand Wheels--30-in. diameter with 1-5/16-in. steel rim.
Tread--Front, 50-inches. Rear, 86-inches.
Wheel Base--164-inches.
Tool Box--13-in. x 36-in. x 6-in.

Scarifier
Total Weight of Scarifier Attachment--1000 pounds.
Weight of Block--260 pounds, cast steel.
Length of Block--44-inches.
Number of Teeth--6.
Size of Teeth--3-in. x 1-in., 21-in. long. Special Carbon Steel.
Spacing Between Teeth--8-1/2-inches.
Lifting Links--1-5/8-in. diameter.
Draw-Bars--4 x 1-1/8-in. Special Carbon Steel.
Scarifier Teeth Clearance--8-inches.
Pitch Adjustment--3 positions.
Back Sloper
Blade for Cutting Ditch Bottom--21-in. long
Wing--46-in. long
Weight--450 pounds.

Caterpillar Thirty pulling a Russell Special Grader. The Special preceded the Super-Special.

Super-Special Grader with optional factory canopy. August 1926.

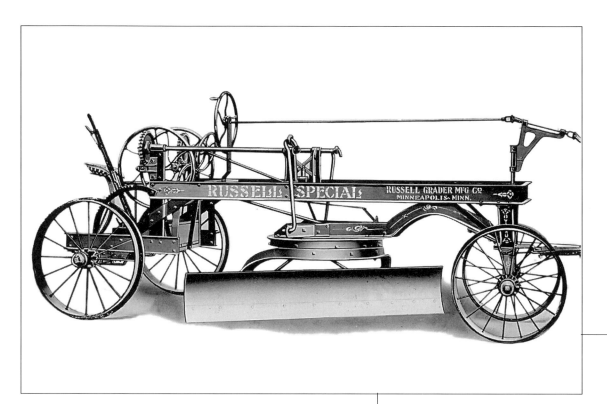

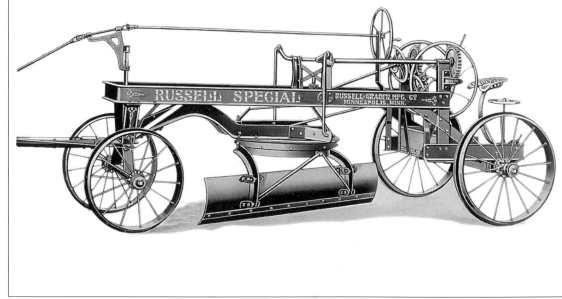

Illustrations of a Russell Special Grader, built from 1912 to 1924.

48

Illustration of the adjustable rear axle on a Special Grader.

RUSSELL SUPER - RELIANCE GRADER

12 - Foot Blade. Weight 7500 Pounds
For 25 Horse Power Tractors.   May also be Equipped with 10 - Foot Blade

Designed for Heavy Grading and Ditching. The Reliance with a 12-foot blade has a capacity equal to or greater than any other grader with the exception of the Super-Mogul. It is built like the Super-Mogul except lighter in weight and will stan up under over-load and rough usage with a minimum of up-keep. **One Mile a Day** of perfectly graded road is possible with the Super-Reliance. In 8 to 12 rounds it will build a 40-foot road with back-sloped, flat bottom ditches 18 inches or more in depth, and the cost is only the daily expense of the engine and the wages of an operator. Scarifier Attachment--Block that replaces the blade may be had for the Super-Reliance Grader. **The Three Point Blade Adjustment** positively makes draft lighter. This adjustment permits the setting of blade in the action of a breaker plow--as well as a stubble plow. In working in rough sod the point of the blade on the Russell Super-Reliance may be placed in a breaker position turning the sod gradually. On no other machine can the blade be placed in a breaker plow position. With this feature we can offer a larger capacity with less power than any other make using the same length blade. **The Spring Blade Lift** enables the operator to raise and lower the blade with ease regardless whether blade is up or down. This Spring Lift also eliminates all blade chatter when grader is used for maintenance work.

Specifications

Blade — Made of special carbon steel.
    Length, 12 feet. Width, 22-1/2 inches.
    Length, 10 feet. Width, 22-1/2 inches.
Moldboard — 10-foot 9/16-in. thick, 12-foot 5/8-in. thick.
Cutting Edge — 2 pieces, 1/2-in. thick.
Blade Beams — 4-in. x 1-1/2-in. solid special carbon steel.
Blade Braces — 1-3/4-in. round.
Blade Pitch Adjustment — Four Positions.
Blade Side Shift — 30 inches.

Blade Lift Above Ground — 15 inches.
Circle — Steel casting, 56-in. diameter, weight 400 lbs.
Draw-Bars — 54-in.x1-in., solid special carbon steel.
Kingbolts — 2-1/4-in. round, special carbon steel.
Frame — 8-in., 16-1/4-lb. channel, reinforced.
Axles — Special carbon cold rolled steel.
    Front, 2-1/2-in. round, 6-ft. 3-in. long.
    Rear, built-up 6-in. section with 2-1/2-in. spindle, 10-ft.
    1-1/2-in. long.
Bearings — 2-1/2-in. x 12-in.

Wheels — Front, 34-in. diameter, 8-in.x1/2-in. tires.
    Rear, 46-in. diameter, 8-in.x1/2-in. tires.
    Detachable flanges of 2-in.x2-in.x3/8-in. angle.
    Removable boxes. Screwed-on hub cap.
Lifting Links--1-5/8-inches round, special carbon steel.
Lifting Arms--2-3/8-inches round, special carbon steel.
Method of Lifting Blade--Worm Gear.
Hand Wheels--43 inches in diameter with 1-3/8-inch steel rim.
Tread--Front, 58 inches. Rear, 106 inches.
Wheel Base--186 inches.
Tool Box--13-in.x36-in.x6-in.

Caterpillar Sixty and Super-Reliance Grader with scarifier. 1928.

Two views of the Russell Reliance equipped with a standard 12-foot blade. The Reliance preceded the Super-Reliance.

52

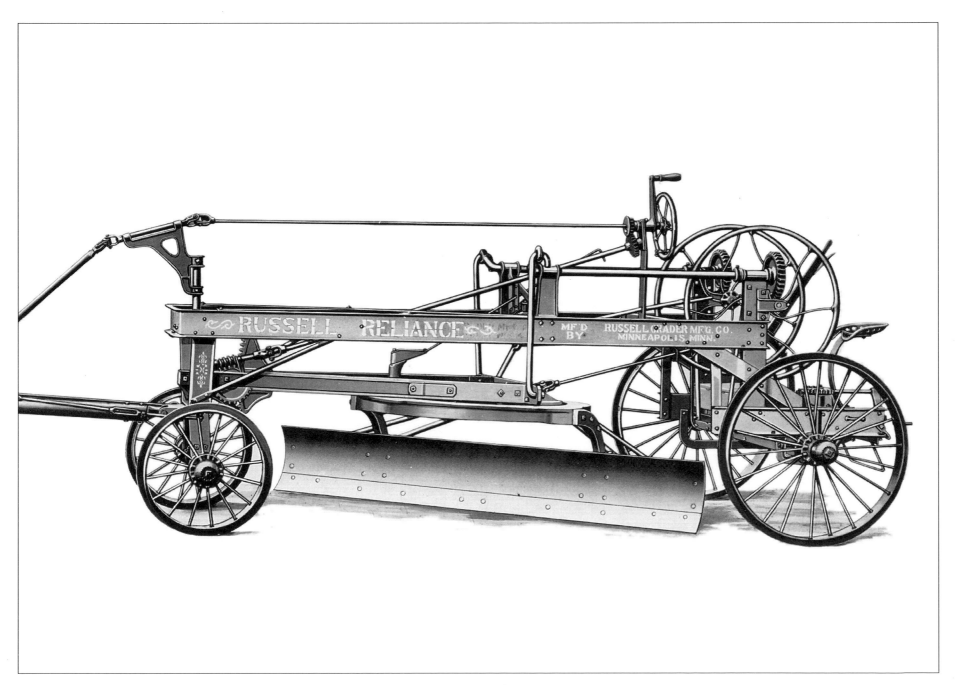

The Reliance preceded the Super-Reliance.

Reliance with scarifier.

54

RUSSELL SUPER - MOGUL GRADER

12 - Foot Blade.   For Tractors of 35 horse power an up.
Weight - without Scarifier, 9,500 Lbs., with Scarifier, 10,200 Lbs.

The Strongest of Them All.--The Super-Mogul is the only road machine equal to the job with the largest tractors. It has the greatest strength and capacity and will build more and better roads at the least expense. **A Powerful Combination Machine**--Scarifier and grader in one unit. The scarifier and blade may be operated together or independently of each other. Tears up gravel, stone or macadam roads with ease. **Scarifier Block** that replaces the blade may also be had for the Super-Mogul Grader. **Designed for a back sloper**--will build a flat bottom ditch 12 inches wide to any greater width desired. **Three-Point Blade Adjustment**--The Draw-bar adjustment with the two regular raising and lowering mechanisms give the Super-Mogul a three point blade adjustment. The moldboard may be set in the action of a breaker plow as well as a stubble plow. **The Spring Blade Lift** consists of a pair of coil springs which are fastened to the front end of frame and power applied over a pair of equalizer cams to the circle. The cams equalize the tension of the springs giving the same lifting power regardless of whether the blade is up or down.

Specifications
Blade — Made of Special Carbon Steel.
      Length, 12 feet. Width, 24 inches.
      Moldboard, 11/16-in. thick.
      Cutting Edge — 1/2-in. thick.
Blade Extension — 3-foot, for right or left side, furnished when
      so ordered.
Blade Beams — 2-in.x4-in. solid special carbon steel.
Blade Braces — 2-in. round.
Blade Pitch Adjustment — 4 positions.
Circle — Steel casting, 66-in. diameter, weight 600 lbs.
Draw-Bars — 5-in.x1-1/4-in.. Solid Special Carbon Steel.
Kingbolt — 2-1/4-in. round, special carbon steel.
Frame — 9-in., 20-lb. channel, reinforced.
Axles — Made of Special Carbon Cold Rolled Steel.
      Front, 2-3/4-in. round, 6-ft. 5-1/2-in. long.
      Rear, built-up 6-in. section with 2-3/4-in. spindle,
      10-ft. 4-3/4-in. long.

Bearings — 2-3/4 inches x 12 inches.
Wheels — Front, 36-in. diameter, 5/8-in. x 8-in. tires.
      Rear, 46-in. diameter, 5/8-in. x 8-in. tires.
      Detachable flanges of 2-in.x2-in.x3/8-in. angle.
      Removable boxes. Screwed-on hub cap.
Lifting Links — 1-5/8-inches round, special carbon steel.
Lifting Arms — 2-3/8-inches round, special carbon steel.
Method of Lifting Blade — Worm Gear. The bronze ring gear may
      be turned or replaced. Both worm and gear are machined
      true. No lost motion.
Hand Wheels — 43 inches in diameter with 1-3/8-inch rims.
Tread — Front, 62 inches. Rear, 109 inches.
Wheel Base — 204 inches.
Tool Box — 13-in.x36-in.x6-in.

Back Sloper
Blade for Cutting Ditch Bottom — 24 inches long.
Wing — 60 inches long.

Weight — 625 pounds.
Scarifier Attachment
Weight of Block — 400 pounds, steel casting.
Length of Block — 52 inches.
Pitch of Block — four positions.
Number of Teeth — 6 — Special carbon steel adjustable vertically
      in block.
Size of Teeth — 3-in. x 1-1/4-in. x 22-1/2-in.
Spacing Between Teeth — 8 inches.
Lifting Links — 2 inches in diameter.
Method of Lifting — Worm gear by mens of hand wheels parallel
with blade lift.
Draw-bars — 1-1/4-in. x 5-in.
Scarifier Block Clearance — 12 inches.

ALWAYS
making them finer

—A well finished job—looks a 100%—shows exactly the kind of work that you can always expect and accomplish with—

RUSSELL
Better Built Road Equipment

Russell constantly plans to build products of higher standard. This process of improvement goes steadily on—creative thinking, careful testing, better designing and finer materials will ever prevail—this is the answer to the remarkable Russell progress.

Our new catalog of special interest to all road builders —sent free and postpaid

Russell Grader Manufacturing Company

Factory and General Offices—Minneapolis, Minn.

Representatives and Warehouses in all principal cities

Deep flat-bottom ditch and perfect slopes, built by Russell Super-Mogal with Back Sloper Attachment

Picture shows finishing the grade—(attachment removed for top finishing)

THE LAST WORD IN ROAD MACHINE CONSTRUCTION

Three Super-Moguls and a Russell Elevating Grader in front of the factory.

Holt Ten-Ton pulling a Super-Mogul Grader.

58

Two views of a Super-Mogul with scarifier. The scarifier weighed 1700 pounds. The entire unit weighed 11,700 pounds.

A Super-Mogul Grader towed by a Caterpillar Sixty at work near Los Banos, California. 1928.

Holt Ten-Ton, Russell Super-Mogul, and an unidentified roller building a rural Minnesota road.

65

Caterpillar Sixty and Super-Mogul Grader cutting brush near Mount Shasta, California. October 1926.

Caterpillar Sixty tractors, a new Russell 60 Grader, and a Super-Mogul Grader on a road job in Illinois. 1929.

Caterpillar Sixty pulling a Super-Mogul Grader near Hill City, South Dakota.

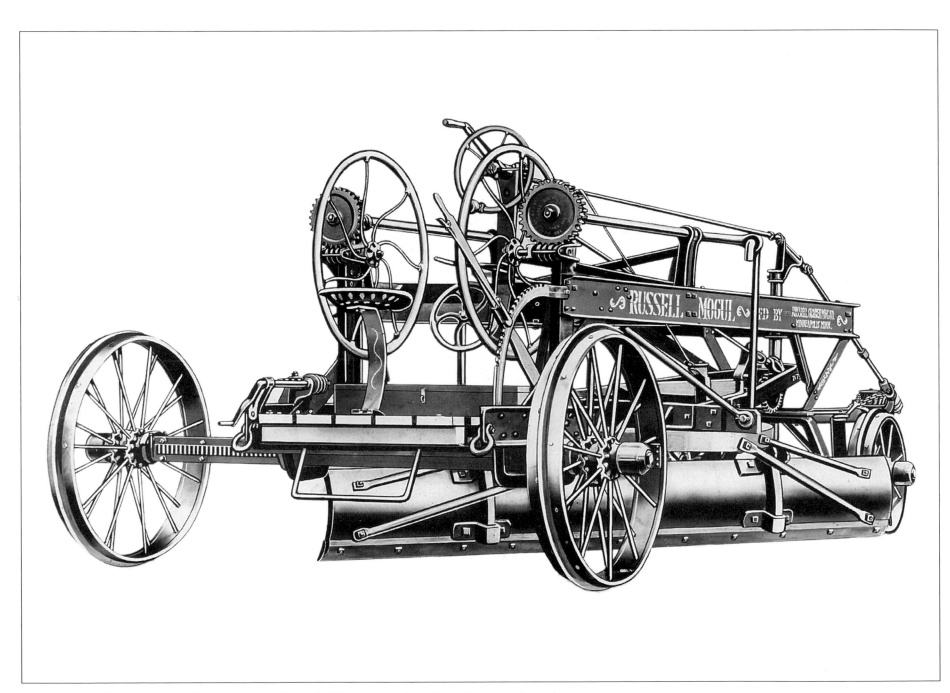

The Russell Mogul, built from 1913 to 1922, preceded the Super Mogul.

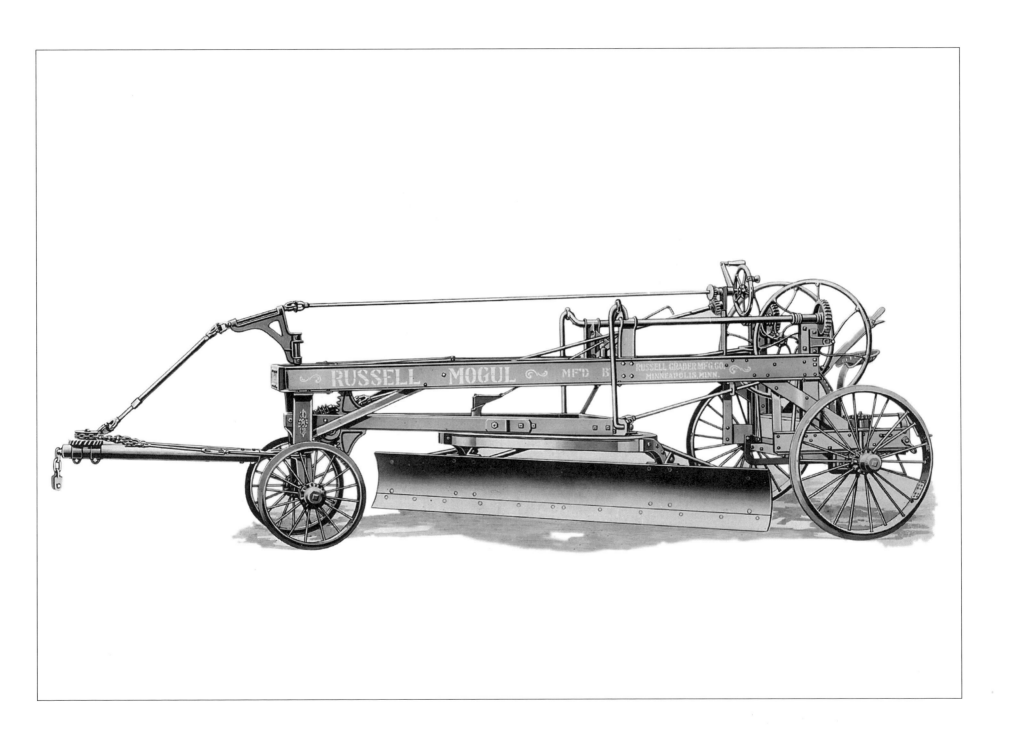

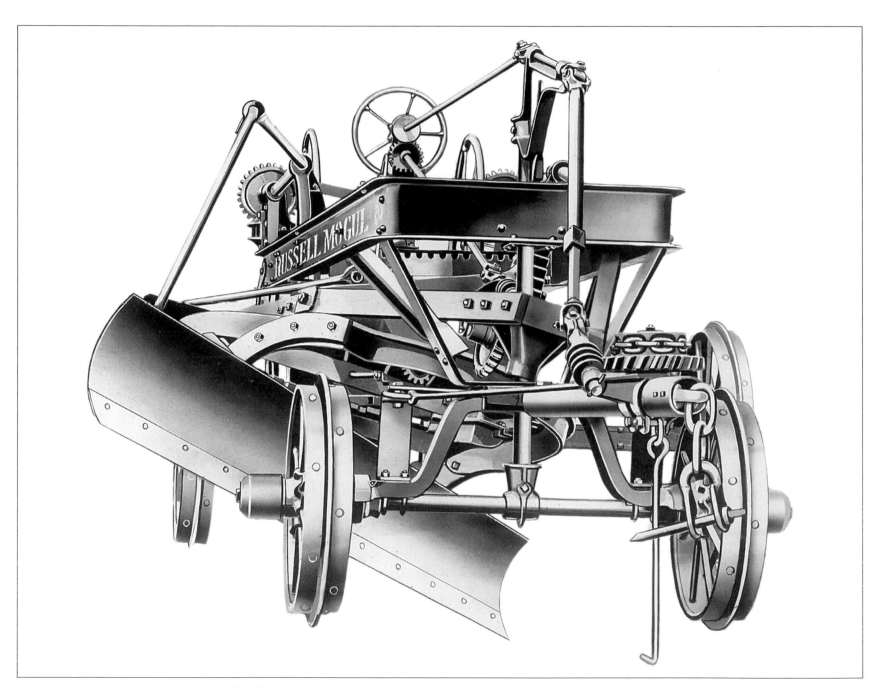

Illustrations showing the shift of the blade on a Mogul Grader.

Case 22-40 pulling a Mogul Grader near Racine, Wisconsin.

Mogul Graders being loaded on to rail cars at the factory.

Russell Model B Elevating Grader pulled by Minneapolis Steel & Machinery Twin City 40.

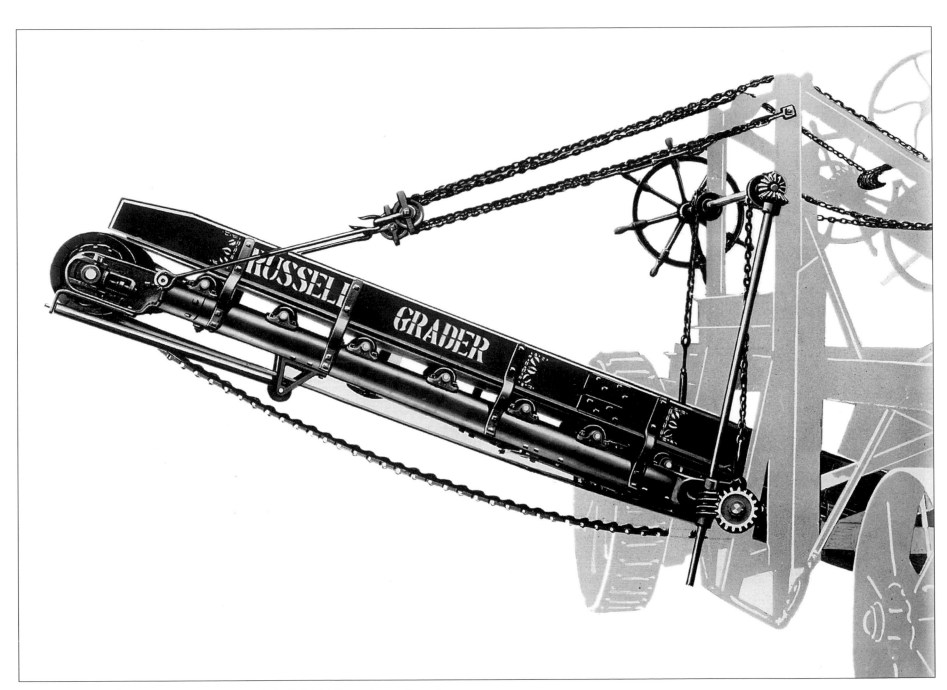

Illustration of the conveyor on a Model B Elevating Grader.

82

Illustration of the Model B Elevating Grader engine steering pole.

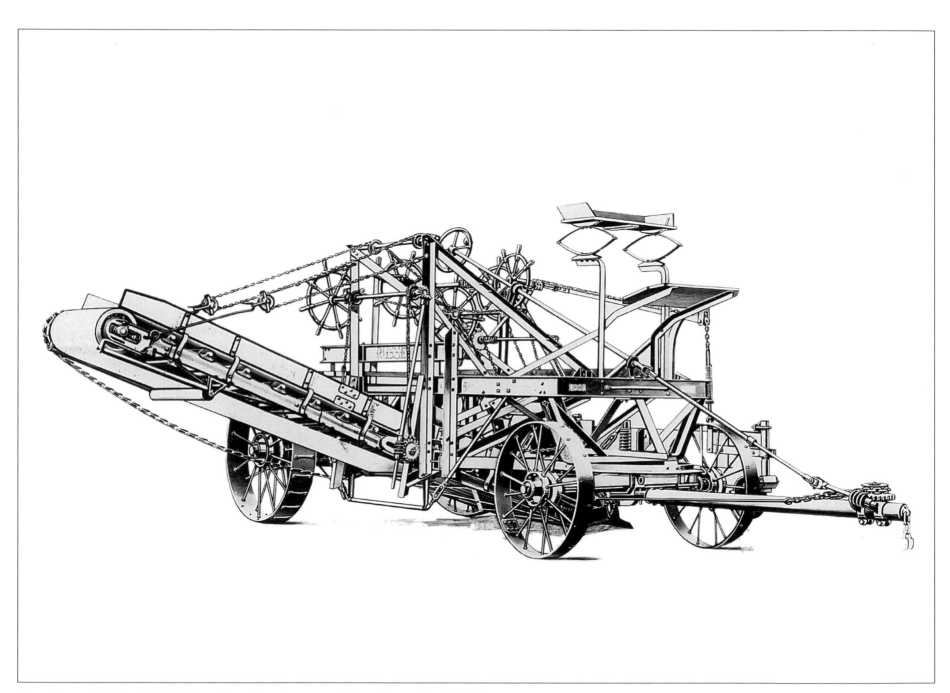

The Russell Model B Elevating Grader was introduced in 1912.

Gas Traction Company Big Four "30" pulling Russell elevating grader.

Russell Model B Elevating Grader pulled by a Holt 25-45.

Frame for a 42-C Elevating Grader. Note gearing and sprocket for transmission of power from the rear drive wheel to the conveyor system. October 1926.

This photo shows the plow beam without a plow attached. Machines were offered with a 12-inch moldboard plow, or choice of rigid or rotary disc plows.

Caterpillar Sixty equipped with experimental rear power take-off, and power operated Russell 42-Giant Elevating Grader.

Three Russell elevating graders working on a Mississippi levee construction project.

Views of a 42 Elevating Grader.

A 42 Elevating Grader from the plow side. Note the position of the moldboard plow relative to the conveyor.

Steel drive wheels for the Model 42 Elevating Grader.

Conveyor drive mechanism for Model 42 Elevating Grader.

Controls for 42 Elevating Grader: (Top) steering; (Lower four, left to right) plow adjustment; carrier hoist lower end; carrier hoist outer end; belt tightener.

Caterpillar Sixty and Russell 42-Giant Elevating Grader leveling ground at a California construction site. June 1928.

Caterpillar Sixty and Russell Sixty Elevating Grader on a road construction site.

Russell Sixty Elevating Grader working with Caterpillar Sixty tractors pulling Athey wagons.

Russell Road Planer pulled by a Twin City 60.

100

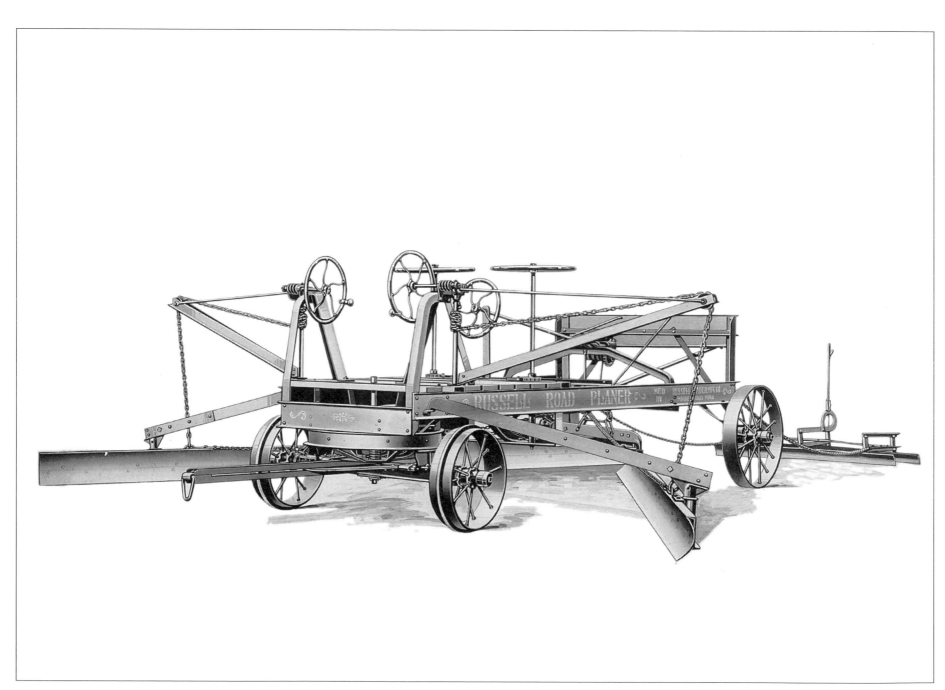

Russell added road planers to its line in 1915.

MOTORIZED GRADERS

Russell Motor Patrol No. 1, engineered from an Allis-Chalmers tractor and a lightweight highway maintainer. 1920.

RUSSELL MOTOR PATROL No. 2
Fordson Tractor for Power

A Better built Motorized Patrol Grader. It meets the growing demand for a more highly finished motorized maintenance grader. It has tight fitting machine-cut gears. Machined bearing with take-up in control connections, more accurate and easy adjustments and a sturdy construction of oversize parts. Built of Oversize Parts, the up-keep is naturally very low. The Russell Motor Patrol will as a result do patrol work at the lowest cost. Independently Adjustable Scarifier. The scarifier and blade may be adjusted or worked separately or simultaneously as desired. The scarifier attachment consists of a steel block on a pair of heavy draw-bars. The ten scarifier teeth of special carbon steel are reversible and adjustable vertically in block. The Long Wheel Base and oversize front wheels insure smooth and uniform work. The weight is distributed so as to give proper balance. Cab is Provided when so ordered. Operator is Stationed in a comfortable position at the rear of the tractor with full view of blade and of the road ahead.

Specifications

Weight Complete With Cab — 8500 pounds.
Weight Without Tractor — 2835 pounds.
Blade — 3 sizes, made of special carbon steel.
    8 foot long regular equipment.
    10 or 12 foot maintenance blade.
Cutting Edge — Made of special carbon steel.
Blade Beams — 3-in.x1-in. flat special carbon steel.
Blade Braces — 1-1/8-inches round.
Blade Pitch Adjustment — 18 degrees.
Blade Side Shift — 8 inches.
Blade Lift Above Ground — 11 inches.
Circle — 3-1/2-in.x3-1/2-in.x1/2-in. "T" shaped.
Draw-Bars — 4-in.x3-in.x1/2" angle.
Method of Blade Lift — Worm gear — cut gears completely enclosed — bronze bushings and collars for worm gear.

Lifting Links — 1-3/8-in. shaft, ball and socket (2-inch steel ball.)
Lifting Arms — 1-3/4-in. shaft, special carbon steel with rake-up bearing in bracket to eliminate play.
Hand Wheels — 30-in. diameter.
Frame — 7-in. extra heavy channel; weight 19-3/4 pounds per foot.
Axle — front — extra heavy — 51 inch tread.
Wheels — Front — 32-in. x 5-in. rubber tires. Timken bearings.
    Rear — 40-in. x 5-in. dual cushion (total width 10 inches).
Steering Control — Worm gear.
Tread — Front — 51 inches.
Wheel Base — 14 feet, 5 inches.

Scarifier Attachment — Independently adjustable; weight 565 lbs.
Width of Block — 40-inches.
Draw-bars for Scarifier — 3-in.x1-in. flat, high carbon.
Size of Teeth — 2-1/2-in.x3/4-in.
Spacing of Teeth — 4-1/8-in. apart.
Number of Teeth — Ten.
Platform Spring Mounted — Checkered plate with steel tool box.
Lubrication — Alemite system — all principal parts. Motor is equipped with governor to insure uniform speed. Side cranking device furnished as regular equipment.

Two views of the Fordson-powered Russell Motor Patrol No. 2.

Two views of a Motor Patrol No. 2 with a factory cab.

Rear view of track-equipped Russell Motor Patrol No. 2.

RUSSELL MOTOR PATROL No. 3

10 - 20 McCormick - Deering Tractor for Power

Cuts Steadier and More Smoothly due to the long wheel base, tight joints and rigid construction. The tight joints prevent chattering and vibration--very essential to good maintenance work. **Built Like the Motor Patrol No. 2**, except some parts are heavier and a McCormick-Deering 10-20 tractor is used for power. **The Better Built** machines are becoming more popular. It costs more to equip with cut and fully machined gears and fully enclose them, bronze bushings, ball and socket connection, independently controlled scarifier and many other features. Russell construction however, will cost less in the end because you are assured of long service with the least upkeep cost. **It Should Also Mean Something** to the Customer that the Motor Patrol is built by a company that has spent many years perfecting and building the most complete line of road grading machinery.

Specifications

Weight Complete with Cab — 10,250 pounds.

Blade — 3 sizes, made of special carbon steel.

    8 Foot long.

    10 Foot blade, regular equipment.

    12 Foot maintenance blade.

Cutting Edge — Made of special carbon steel.

Blade Beams — 3-1/2x1-1/4-inches flat special carbon steel.

Blade Braces — 1-1/8-inches round.

Blade Pitch Adjustment — 4 positions.

Blade Side Shift — 12 inches.

Blade Lift Above Ground — 12 inches.

Circle — 52-inch diameter, 4x4x1/2-inch "T" Steel.

Draw-Bars — 5x3x3/8-inch angle.

Method of Blade Lift — Worm gear — cut gears completely enclosed — bronze bushings and collars for worm gear.

Lifting Links — 1-3/8-in. shaft, ball and socket (2-inch steel ball.)

Lifting Arms — 1-7/8-in. shaft, special carbon steel with rake-up bearing in bracket to eliminate play.

Hand Wheels — 30-in. diameter.

Frame — 7-in. extra heavy channel; weight 19-3/4 pounds per foot.

Axle — Front, extra heavy — 51 inches long.

Wheels — Front — 32x5 inch rubber tires. Timken bearings.

    Rear — 40x5 dual cushion, (total width 10 inches).

Steering control — Worm gear.

Tread — Front, 51 inches.

Wheel Base — 16 feet, 2 inches.

Scarifier Attachment — Independently adjustable.

Weight of Scarifier — 700 pounds.

Width of Block — 48 inches.

Draw-bars for Scarifier — 3-1/2x1-1/4 inches flat bars.

Size of Teeth — 2-1/2x3/4 inch.

Spacing of teeth — 4 inches apart.

Number of Teeth — 12.

Platform — Size 28x38 inches, checkered plate, spring mounted.

Lubrication — Alemite system-all principal parts. Motor is equipped with governor to insure uniform speed. Side cranking device furnished as regular equipment.

A line of Motor Patrol No. 3 graders in the assembly area. A McCormick-Deering 10-20 tractor was used for power. March 1926.

Motor Patrol No. 3 with snow plow. November 1926.

Close-up of the Motor Patrol No. 3 blade and scarifier. A 10-foot blade was standard; 8 and 12-foot blades were offered. March 1927.

Front steering linkage on the Motor Patrol No. 3.

Side cranking device as fitted to the Motor Patrol No. 3.

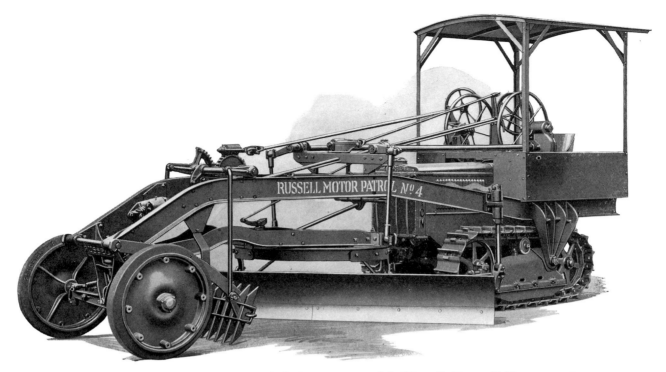

RUSSELL MOTOR PATROL No. 4
Caterpillar Two - Ton Tractor for Power

This Motorized Grader is built for heavy maintenance work on gravel or earth roadways. It is capable of working in loose or sandy soil where wheel type tractors could not be used. The operator's station is at rear of machine where he has an unobstructed view of the road ahead as well as that of the blade. The steering mechanism is similar to the wheel type motor graders. The unit is very easily handled, has plenty of power, and the entire outfit is most sturdily built. The many improved features found on this machine insures economy, service, and a lower up-keep cost. The grader unit can be mounted on the tractor with very little difficulty.

Specifications
Grader Unit
Weight (Grader unit only) — without scarifier 3800 pounds, with scarifier 4500 pounds.
The Blade is reversible and may be tilted forward or backward from a leveling to a cutting position. Offered in 3 sizes:
> 12-foot long (regular equipment).
> 10-foot long.
> 8-foot long.

Blade Pitch Adjustment — 4 positions.
Blade Lift Above Ground — 12 inches.
Blade Side Shift — 18 inches. The lateral shift of blade, allows the blade to be moved to either side of the main frame.
Draw-Bars — 5x3x1/2-inch angle.
Method of Blade Lift — Machine cut gears completely enclosed — bronze bushings and collars for worm gear. Extra large ball and socket connections in lift lints.

Hand Wheels — 30-in. diameter.
Frame — 7-in. extra heavy channel; weight 19-3/4 pounds per foot.
Axle — Front, extra wide — 51 inch spread.
Wheels — Front — 32x5 inch rubber tires. Timken bearings.
Steering Control — Worm gear.
Tread — Front, 51 inches.
Wheel Base — 16 feet, 2 inches.
Scarifier Attachment — Independently adjustable.
Weight of Scarifier — 700 pounds.
Width of Block — 48 inches.
Draw-bars for Scarifier — 3-1/2x1-1/4 inches.
Size of Teeth — 2-1/2x3/4 inch.
Spacing of teeth — 4 inches apart.
Number of Teeth — 12.
Lubrication — Alemite system — all principal parts.

A Steel Cab is Provided. It is practically weather proof when side curtains are attached. The side curtains are not regularly included but are furnished when so ordered.
Motive Power
> A Two-Ton Caterpillar Tractor.

Speeds — first, 2-1/8 mile per hour; second, 3 miles per hour; third, 5-1/4 miles per hour; reverse, 2-3/8 miles per hour.
Motor Power — 25 H. P.
Drawbar Power — 15 H. P.
Width of Track — 10-1/2 inches.
Ground Contact of Tracks — 51 inches, spread out side to outside — 48 inches.
Motor — 4 cylinder, overhead valve, 4 inch bore, 5-1/2 inch stroke, speed 1000 R. P. M.
To remove tractor from grader requires pulling two pins and removing six bolts.

RUSSELL
Better Built
Road Equipment

RUSSELL
Motor Patrol
Builds Better Roads for the
PRESIDENT

Brule, Wisconsin got a big surprise and the village with its surrounding territory played in big luck in being chosen for President Coolidge's summer home. Just another touch of good luck is due to the fact that the road leading from Brule to Superior is being maintained with a—

RUSSELL NO. 4 MOTOR PATROL
With "CATERPILLAR" 2-TON TRACTOR for Power

This machine demonstrates unusual fitness and capacity in keeping roads in fine shape regardless of the weather. Wherever road construction and road maintenance is being carried on at its best you'll find Russell Equipment predominates.

The complete Russell Line for Road Construction, and Road Maintenance includes—
4 Sizes Motorized (Unified) Road Machines
10 Sizes Road Machines (for Horse or Tractor Power)
3 Sizes Elevating Graders

*Scarifiers, Road Drags and Wheel Scrapers, Drag Lines, Conveyors, Gravel
Screening, Crushing and Loading Equipment, etc.*

Our new catalog of special interest to all road builders—sent free and postpaid

Russell Grader Manufacturing Co.

Factory and General Offices:
Minneapolis, Minnesota

The Gateway to Brule

Maintaining Road Leading to Brule

Showing Real Russell Capacity

A Motor Patrol No. 4 with standard 12-foot blade and optional snow plow attachment. February 1927.

Two views of the Caterpillar Two-Ton powered Motor Patrol No. 4. November 1926.

Motor Patrol frame and front axle assembly, as fitted to the Caterpillar Two-Ton.

Front and rear views of the Cletrac K-20 powered Motor Patrol No. 5. 1927.

Two views of a Russell Fifteen Motor Patrol. It used a Caterpillar Fifteen tractor for power.

The Motor Patrol No. 6, built on the Caterpillar Twenty tractor, was introduced in August 1928. A 12-foot blade was standard.

In 1927, as an experiment, Russell built the first motorized grader with hydraulically operated blade.

Russell Drag Line. April 1926.

Waukesha engine used on the Russell Drag Line.

Scale model used to develop the Russell Drag Line.

The Drag Line 60 was fitted with a Twin City Tractor engine.

Russell dump wagon.

Russell 21-yard storage bin.

Russell No. 10 plant, the industry's first portable gravel screening and crushing plant.

Russell Screening, Crushing and Loading Plant No. 20. In 1929, Caterpillar sold the gravel equipment line to a group of Russell employees.

Grader Serial Numbers: This list was prepared by Caterpillar Tractor Co. in June 1929. It included all serial numbers used to that date for graders manufactured by Russell Grader Mfg. Co. or Caterpillar. In the case of motor graders, this list refers only to the grader serial number, and not to that of the tractor itself.

GRADER SERIAL NUMBER	MODEL	YEAR MANUFACTURED	LOCATION OF NUMBER PLATE
A-1 to A-364	Unassigned		
A-365 to A-538	"A" Elev. Grader	1912 to 1915	Main Frame, Left Side
A-539 to A-575	"A" Elev. Grader	1915	Main Frame, Left Side
A-576 to A-644	"A" Elev. Grader	1915 to 1916	Main Frame, Left Side
A-645 to A-840	"A" Elev. Grader	1916 to 1921	Main Frame, Left Side
B-1 to B-364	Unassigned		
B-365 to B-538	"B" Elev. Grader	1912 to 1916	Main Frame, Left Side
B-539 to B-575	"B" Elev. Grader	1915	Main Frame, Left Side
B-576 to B-644	"B" Elev. Grader	1915 to 1916	Main Frame, Left Side
B-645 TO B-905	"B" Elev. Grader	1916 to 1922	Main Frame, Left Side
B-906 to B-960	"B" Elev. Grader	1922 to 1925	Main Frame, Left Side
B-961 and Up	"B" Elev. Grader	1926 to Date	Main Frame, Left Side
BH-1 to BH-654	Unassigned		
BH-655 to BH-809	"B" Heavy Elev. Grader	1917 to 1921	Main Frame, Left Side
BH-810 to BH-875	"42-C" Elev. Grader	1922 to 1924	Main Frame, Left Side
BH-876 to BH-995	"42-C" Elev. Grader	1924 to 1926	Main Frame, Left Side
BH-996 to BH-1170	"42-C" Elev. Grader	1926 to 1929	Main Frame, Left Side
BH-1171 and Up	"42-C" Elev. Grader	1929 to Date	Main Frame, Left Side
D-1 to D-1000	Unassigned		
D-1001 to D-1500	Standard No. 2	1926 to 1928	Main Frame, Left Side
D-1501 and Up	Standard No. 2	1928 to Date	Main Frame, Left Side
E-1 to E-100	Unassigned		
E-101 to E-1200	Standard No. 1 (Badger)	1924 to 1929	Main Frame, Right Side
E-1201 and Up	Russell Ten Grader	1929 to Date	Main Frame, Left Side
G-1 to G-1000	Gem	1916 to 1919	No record
G-1001 to G-1150	Gem	1920	Cross Channel, Under Seat
G-1151 to G-1575	Gem	1920 to 1925	Cross Channel, Under Seat
G-1576 to G-2000	Unassigned		
G-2001 to G-2800	Hi-Way Patrol No. 3	1926 to 1928	Main Frame, Left Side
G-2801 and Up	Hi-Way Patrol No. 3	1928 to Date	Main Frame, Left Side

GRADER SERIAL NUMBER	MODEL	YEAR MANUFACTURED	LOCATION OF NUMBER PLATE
42G-1 to 42G-100	Unassigned		
42G-101 to 42G-152	42-Giant Elev. Grader	1927	Main Frame, Left Side
42G-153 to 42G-200	42-Giant Elev. Grader	1927 to 1928	Main Frame, Left Side
42G-201 and Up	42-Giant Elev. Grader	1928 to Date	Main Frame, Left Side
H-1 to H-2000	Hi-Way Patrol	1918 to 1920	Cross Channel, Under Seat
H-2001 to H-3500	Hi-Way Patrol	1920 to 1922	Cross Channel, Under Seat
H-3501 to H-4375	Hi-Way Patrol	1922 to 1923	Cross Channel, Under Seat
H-4376 to H-9275	Hi-Way Patrol No. 2	1923 to 1926	Main Frame, Right Side
H-9276 to H-10875	Hi-Way Patrol No. 2	1927 to 1929	Main Frame, Right Side
IP-1 to IP-100	Unassigned		
IP-101 to IP-168	Motor Patrol No. 3	1926	Main Frame, Left Side
IP-169 to IP-300	Motor Patrol No. 3	1926 to 1927	Main Frame, Left Side
IP-301 to IP-500	Motor Patrol No. 3	1927 to 1928	Main Frame, Left Side
IP-501 to IP-587	Motor Patrol No. 3	1928	Main Frame, Left Side
IP-588 to IP-750	Motor Patrol No. 3	1928 to 1929	Main Frame, Left Side
J-1 to J-6475	Junior	1912 to 1923	Main Frame, Right Side
J-6476 and Up	Junior	1923 to Date	Main Frame, Right Side
K-1 and Up	Sixty Elev. Grader	1929 to Date	Main Frame, Left Side
M-1 to M-49	Unassigned		
M-50 to M-361	Mogul	1913 to 1915	Main Frame, Front
M-362 to M-1446	Mogul	1915 to 1922	Main Frame, Left Side
M-1447 to M-2196	Super-Mogul	1922 to 1927	Main Frame, Left Side
M-2197 to M-2500	Super-Mogul	1927 to 1928	Main Frame, Left Side
M-2501 and Up	Super-Mogul	1928 to Date	Main Frame, Left Side
P-1 to P-100	Unassigned		
P-101 to P-125	Pony Patrol	1921 to 1922	Cross Channel, Under Seat
P-126 to P-2425	(Pony Patrol)		
	(Russell Patrol)		
	(Hi-Way Patrol No. 1)	1922 to 1929	Main Frame, Left Side
R-1 to R-49	Unassigned		
R-50 to R-1100	Reliance	1915 to 1923	Main Frame, Left Side
R-1101 to R-1450	Super-Reliance	1923 to 1928	Main Frame, Left Side

GRADER SERIAL NUMBER	MODEL	YEAR MANUFACTURED	LOCATION OF NUMBER PLATE
R-1451 to R-1500	Unassigned		
R-1501 and Up	Super-Reliance	1929 to Date	Main Frame, Left Side
S-1 to S-500	Unassigned		
S-501 to S-1000	Standard Reversible	1908 to 1912	Main Frame, Right Side
S-1001 to S-4950	Standard	1912 to 1925	Main Frame, Left Side
S-4951 to S-6000	Standard No. 3	1925 to 1928	Main Frame, Left Side
S-6001 and Up	Standard No. 3	1928 to Date	Main Frame, Left Side
T-1 to T-100	Unassigned		
T-101 to T-200	Motor Patrol No. 2	1925	(Frame Cross Member
T-201 to T-450	Motor Patrol No. 2	1925 to 1928	at Front of Platform)
T-451 to T-500	Unassigned		
T-501 to T-1000	Traction Special	1908 to 1912	Main Frame, Left Side
T-1001 to T-2000	Unassigned		
T-2001 to T-5999	Special	1912 to 1924	Main Frame, Left Side
T-6000 to T-6100	Super-Special	1924	Main Frame, Left Side
T-6101 to T-6399	Super-Special	1924 to 1925	Main Frame, Left Side
T-6400 to T-7500	Super-Special	1925 to 1928	Main Frame, Left Side
T-7501 and Up	Super-Special	1928 to Date	Main Frame, Left Side
U-1 to U-100	Unassigned		
U-101 to U-150	Motor Patrol No. 4	1926	(Frame Cross Member
U-151 to U-425	Motor Patrol No. 4	1926 to 1928	at Front of Platform)
U-426 to U-552	Motor Patrol No. 4	1928	" "
U-553 to U-750	Motor Patrol No. 4	1928 to 1929	" "
V-1 to V-100	Unassigned		
V-101 to V-150	Motor Patrol No. 5	1927	(Frame Cross Member
V-151 to V-250	Motor Patrol No. 5	1927 to 1929	at Front of Platform)
X-1 to X-100	Unassigned		
X-101 and Up	(Motor Patrol No. 6)		
	(Twenty Motor Patrol)	1928 to Date	Main Frame, Left Side
Y-1 and Up	Fifteen Motor Patrol	1929 to Date	Main Frame, Left Side
Z-1 and Up	Ten Motor Patrol	1929 to Date	Main Frame, Left Side

The Iconografix Photo Archive Series includes:

JOHN DEERE MODEL D Photo Archive	ISBN 1-882256-00-X
JOHN DEERE MODEL B Photo Archive	ISBN 1-882256-01-8
FARMALL F-SERIES Photo Archive	ISBN 1-882256-02-6
FARMALL MODEL H Photo Archive	ISBN 1-882256-03-4
CATERPILLAR THIRTY Photo Archive	ISBN 1-882256-04-2
CATERPILLAR SIXTY Photo Archive	ISBN 1-882256-05-0
TWIN CITY TRACTOR Photo Archive	ISBN 1-882256-06-9
MINNEAPOLIS-MOLINE U-SERIES Photo Archive	ISBN 1-882256-07-7
HART-PARR Photo Archive	ISBN 1-882256-08-5
OLIVER TRACTOR Photo Archive	ISBN 1-882256-09-3
HOLT TRACTORS Photo Archive	ISBN 1-882256-10-7
RUSSELL GRADERS Photo Archive	ISBN 1-882256-11-5

The Iconografix Photo Archive Series is available from direct mail specialty book dealers and bookstores throughout the world, or can be ordered from the publisher.

For information write to:

Iconografix
P.O. Box 609   or
Osceola, Wisconsin 54020

Telephone: (715) 294-2792
(800) 289-3504 (US and Canada only)
Fax: (715) 294-3414